No Village Too Far

My Journey as a Missionary

a memoir

Dorretta Brown

with Linda Scheele

No Village Too Far

Copyright © 2009 by Dorretta Brown

ISBN: 1-4776-4856-9

ISBN-13: 9781477648568

Dedicated to Zeral L. Brown

Acknowledgments

I dedicate this book to my late husband, Zeral L. Brown. He taught me everything I know. He was multi-talented and worldly wise and I was a country girl that had never made it out of the state of Minnesota until I married. He was my Bible and my teacher in all things spiritual and non-spiritual. He loved to read and to preach and was knowledgeable in so many areas. Together we learned to live by faith, trusting God to supply all our needs in every area of life. After 12 years of being without him, I miss him more every day.

I give all the credit for this book to Linda Scheele. It was her encouragement and help that gave me the impulse I needed to write down my experiences. She took the humble and poorly written words and arranged them in readable and understandable language. I hope you enjoy my story and that as you read it you will be challenged to follow God's will for your life.

Table of Contents

Zeral and Dorretta Brown with their two kids, Joanna and Philip

Prologue

*Be anxious for nothing; but in
everything by prayer and supplication
with thanksgiving let your requests be
made known to God. And the peace of
God, which passeth all understanding,
shall keep your hearts and minds
through Christ Jesus.*

Philippians 4:6-7

60 years as a missionary . . . who would have thought this timid little tow-headed girl, born on a farm in southern Minnesota, the seventh in a family of ten, would ever arrive at this point!

It was May 1, 1947 when my husband, Zeral, and I left Fort Wayne, Indiana in a '35 Ford with our two small children for the Dominican Republic. We drove our car to Miami and spent three days in a hotel while Zeral took care of all the business matters: shipping our car, sending boxes and crates by boat, getting visas, tickets, and so forth.

1

Then we boarded a prop plane and flew to the Dominican Republic, stopping at Camagüey, Cuba, and then again at Port-au-Prince, Haiti, and finally arriving in Santo Domingo that afternoon. I dreaded the trip on the plane with my little one-year old boy, as he was very active. However, he went to sleep and slept the whole way through, even during the stops in Cuba and Haiti.

What a strange place it was! We didn't know the language. We didn't know the people. We'd never been here before. We were met by Lyle and Marie Jesup (another missionary family), who took us to their home in a little village called "El Seibo" in the eastern part of the Island. We lived with them for several months.

I remember waking up the first morning to strange noises, drum-like sounds and then a lot of chattering. I learned later that the drum sounds came from the donkeys being led to the river, carrying big square tin cans on each side used to bring water up for the families. There was no running water in town. And the chattering came from the people in the streets, speaking Spanish. It sounded like what I imagine monkeys would sound like. The only electricity in town was the city generator, which was turned on only at dusk. Mosquitoes were prolific, especially at night. I have counted as many as 35 bites on one leg. We ate dinner in the evening with our legs wrapped in our housecoats. Malaria was very common at that time.

The Jesups were trying to start a church in the town but the going was hard. Seibo is known for its hard hearts. The Jesups had two little boys, so our children had playmates immediately. Lyle Jesup began Spanish lessons for us.

After a few months, we rented a house on a street called "Palo Hincado." The literal translation was "kneeling stick" but to the locals it actually meant "crooked street." For the first time since my children were born, I felt like I could let go of their hands because we were in our own home. The house was owned by a large Arab family, who lived behind us. They kept pigs in their backyard. Our bathroom facility was a privy in the yard, only a few feet from the house. We shared the building with the neighbors. A fence ran right down the center of the building to separate us from them.

The former renters kept fighting cocks in the house, so we hired some people to clean it and gave them money for soap and supplies. We found out the money was spent—but no soap was bought. A fresh coat of paint covered a lot. After furnishing our home with some new and some borrowed furniture, I felt like a queen in a palace, in my own home at last. Using kerosene lamps and not having running water or an inside bathroom were not new to me. In fact, I was reminded so much of home that it almost made me homesick.

Life on the Farm

*For you created my inmost being; you
knit me together in my mother's womb.*

Psalm 139:13

I'm so glad that God prepared me for missionary life. Being born and raised on a farm, one of ten children, I had to do many things. We had no electricity and no running water. My brothers and sisters and I would walk to a small country school in a little crossroads called "Grogan," and then we would walk the mile home. In the wintertime, we would often take the sleigh because of the heavy snows. We would sit on straw bedding, covered over with a wool blanket, and the horses would pull the sleigh to the school. Sometimes we had to stop along the way and our brothers would have to shovel snow, so the horses could get through. I can remember arriving at the schoolhouse some mornings even before the teacher got there, because of the storms, and having to start the big furnace in order to keep warm.

We had lots of chores to do every day to keep the farm running. Every morning and every night, we would help our brothers milk the cows. Each evening as the older kids were coming in from the field work, the younger ones would go after the cows down a long lane and drive them home. When I was attending high school, I got to choose whether I would milk the cows in the morning or the evening; my sister and I took turns.

We would have to carry in firewood for the wood-burning cook stove that we used in the kitchen. And sometimes we would gather corn cobs off the ground where the pigs had been eating the corn, in order to start the fires in the early morning.

At a very early age, we learned to carry water from the pump house to the house. I can remember that we started out with a little half-gallon pail and then as we grew older, we used a gallon pail. And, as we got stronger, we each carried a 3-gallon pail of water. Later, we filled 5-gallon pails, put them in a wagon and pushed and pulled it to the house to fill the reservoir on the stove and the water bucket for drinking. All of this was good training for me in my future life as a missionary. Even today, women in many of the villages of the Dominican

Republic still carry water in 5-gallon buckets on their heads.

And just like me, when I was a child, many of their children begin by carrying smaller pails of water.

Living on the farm, we grew and canned a lot of our vegetables. In later years, my sister, Evalyn wrote a book of poetry and included this verse in one of her poems:

> Remember shelling peas at night?
> Or stemming beans outside on the lawn,
> All ready for Mother to can the next day?
> She was ready to go before dawn.

Excerpt from "Memories" by Evalyn Peters

I started learning to cook very early—and I loved cooking—and still do. I learned to bake bread in 4-H clubs, and learned to sew and make my own clothes. And it wasn't long before I was making the clothes for my younger sisters. Sometimes we didn't have money to buy fabric, but our aunts from another state would send us their used clothes. I would pick them apart at the seams and iron them, lay them out on the table surface, pin patterns to them, and make clothes for us. There were four younger girls in our family. Evalyn was the oldest. And then there were two younger than I, Stella and Aldine.

When I was 10 years old, a family from the town of St. James came out to our little country school and offered a daily vacation Bible school. Vacation Bible school was something new to us. We learned the verses, won some prizes, and heard the stories. Though we didn't attend church regularly, mother would take us in the summer—on nice days. If anything else came up, we didn't go because church was not a priority. So we didn't get the training that we could have gotten if we had attended faithfully.

The same family who brought the vacation Bible school to our town invited an evangelist to come speak. All of the parents and neighbors were invited to come hear the evangelist preach in the evening. One night, my older sister, who was 6 years older than I (16, at the time), went forward after the meeting and received Jesus Christ as her Savior. I was surprised and puzzled about what she did and watched her in her daily life after that. We didn't know . . . I didn't know . . . what happened to my sister that night. But whatever it was, as I watched her daily, I decided it's not what I wanted. It's not for me. She would sit around reading her Bible and she didn't look very happy. She didn't want to go out with our friends anymore to house parties, play cards, or dance. She started letting her hair grow long and rolled it in a bun. The only friends she had were of the persuasion that it was what they had to do to please the Lord. So I kept saying, "No, no, that's not for me." But Ila was faithful. She continued to serve the Lord. And in another couple of years, when she heard about a Bible school in Minneapolis, she decided that was what she wanted to do. She moved up to Minneapolis and started going to Bible school. Every time she came home for holidays, she would talk to us and read Bible stories. She crawled in bed with us at night—with a family that large and only four bedrooms we had to kind of double up. She would tell us how we needed to know Jesus. But we were not concerned about it and we didn't heed her plea. Sometimes when she was home, we would go to church with her. As they were taking communion, I can remember my brother and me making fun of her, saying, "She's getting drunk in church" or "she's drinking wine." I wonder sometimes what the Lord thought about us.

On another occasion, I was talking to my mom and I asked her, "Mom, what would you think if all your girls did what Ila was doing? Would that make you happy?" She answered, "No . . . no, I don't think so. I just want you all to be happy." She seemed to have the same impression that I had about Ila not being very happy.

Later when I graduated from high school, I decided that I wanted more than what this little town had to offer. I wanted to go to the big city where my sister was living. She told me, "If you want to come, I'll get a job in a home for you." The only thing that I knew how to do was to cook and sew and clean. And she was able to find me that kind of job. I thought, "Oh, now I'm going to get to go to the big nightclubs and dances and movie houses, and I will be really happy." But I was just a little country girl. I was timid. I didn't know anybody except my sister. And the only place she ever went was church. Since I had no other places to go, I would go along with her. I lasted one month visiting church every Sunday evening and every Thursday evening before I felt moved by the Holy Spirit to go forward and accept Jesus as my Savior. Then the battle began. Satan really fought for my soul during those days. I tossed and turned at night and thought to myself, "Oh, if I just hadn't gone forward that night, nobody would know and I could go back and live like I wanted to live and do the things I wanted to do. Why did I have to go in front of people so that they knew?" It wasn't long after that that I made a visit home over the weekend. That Saturday night, my sister and my brothers were all going out to this roadhouse. I wanted to go along but I didn't have a fancy dress to wear so I borrowed one from my sister. We went to the dance. As I danced and watched the people, I thought to myself, "Oh no, I am not in the place God wants me to be." And I was a most unhappy person. I remember going outside and talking to my girlfriend and finally telling her, "I do not belong here. I'm not happy here. I'm a Christian; I received Jesus as my Savior and I don't feel good about being here." Early the next morning, I was talking to my mom as she cooked breakfast. I told her about the previous night and how unhappy it made me and I said, "I was saved in Minneapolis and I should never have gone to that dance." And mom said, "I know, your sister told me." Then I was doubly ashamed that I had had such a bad testimony before my family.

Over time my love for God grew as I studied His Word. My only desire was to obey him.

"D" and "Z": Our Early Years

Two are better than one, because
they have a good return for their
work.

Ecclesiastes 4:9

It was soon after my visit home that I decided to
go to Bible school and learn a little bit more about what I
believed and about the faith that I professed. My sister
was in Bible school and was just graduating from
Seminary, so I enrolled in her Bible school. There I met
so many other young people who loved the Lord and
were following Him. And they were happy people who
really wanted to serve Him. It was that first year, while
standing in line registering for the second semester, that
a young man named Zeral Brown came up to the group I
was with and started talking and telling Bible jokes—
little things like, "who is the shortest man in the Bible?"
Of course, the answer was "knee-high Miah"
(Nehemiah), who was only knee high. Evidently he was
attracted to me and I was so thrilled to think someone

was taking notice of me. Zeral was the president of our freshman class. He was a talented man who sang in a quartet and also sang in a choir group. He was often a speaker for our class. I was thrilled to think that this young man would take notice of me—a little country girl. We often met in the hall after that to stop and talk.

Both Zeral and I had first enrolled in Bible school in the fall of 1941. He had to register for the draft at that time, but because of a deformed leg (from an injury when he was about 13 or 14 years old), he was deferred. So he didn't have to go to war and was able to finish school, which was not the case with many of our student friends. I can well remember the day when the news came over the air that the Japanese airplanes flew over Honolulu and bombed our naval site there. It was such an incredible tragedy and a lot of mourning went on at our Bible school.

We continued to get acquainted and then on March 29th we had our very first date. He asked me to go with him to another church where they were having a concert of some sort. I really don't remember the details but I remember that I was thrilled. Soon after that there was the upcoming spring banquet and he asked me to go with him as his date. Oh, that was so exciting. But I really didn't have anything suitable to wear to a banquet. The lady that I worked for in the home where I lived had a dress that she said I could have altered. She even had her seamstress make a little jacket to go with it. And so she fixed me up and that's what I wore to the banquet that spring.

After the banquet, in our class on Personal Evangelism, we were asked about our summer plans.

We were offered—not only offered, but encouraged—to go out and teach in daily vacation Bible schools or camps. There were lots of requests for workers (Bible school students) who would like to come and help. I volunteered to go to a place in Willmar, Minnesota, where I taught vacation Bible school. Zeral went to Bemidji, Minnesota, to a camp where he was a counselor and worked with boys.

On May 14, 1942, before we left to go out to teach Bible school, Zeral asked me to marry him. We had just gotten off a bus. He led me to a park bench and he got down on his knee and proposed! When we got back from working all summer, we went shopping and picked out a small diamond ring together. We were so excited!

About six weeks into the summer, when daily vacation Bible school and camps were over, Zeral's parents traveled all the way from Washington State in a little old Willy's car. They picked us up and took us all the way back across the northern part of the United States to Washington, where we got jobs to earn our fall tuition. My first trip out of the state of Minnesota was very memorable. We went through the Black Hills and

— then saw Yellowstone National Park and all the scenery and mountains on the way. What an experience for me!

We each got a job when we arrived in Washington. I went to work in a drug store serving food at a lunch counter. Zeral got a job at the Bremerton Shipyards. It was a government job. They were paying good salaries for workers, even though they really didn't need them. He would come home from work and the only dirt on his outfit was where he put his hands on his hips, standing around most of the day. I, on the other hand, was serving food and working hard. His weekly paycheck was $51, while mine was $21—that was pretty hard to take!

At the end of the summer when it was time to go back to school and start our classes, we didn't have a way back. Those were the years of World War II and so there was a crunch on. Someone suggested that we put an ad in the paper. People were driving back and forth all the time and, in order to save on gas, they were looking for passengers. So we found a man who was driving back across the states in a nice, big car. We each paid him our share and he drove us all the way back to Minneapolis, Minnesota.

We signed up for the fall semester and went through the next school year dating as often as we could. Zeral would make choir trips to the different states and back again, and always he would write me a card every day. All that winter we would meet on weekends and whenever we could. It was COLD in Minnesota. Sometimes we would go out and sit on the very park bench where he proposed to me, in our overcoats and our boots, and our heads all covered up, and try to hold hands with gloves on . . . with snow all around us.

We got special permission from the school that winter to be married in the spring, because it was against the rules to be married before graduation. We were married June 6, 1943. We pooled our money to save up enough to buy all of the things necessary for a little wedding. We planned to have the wedding in the home of one of our professors (a pastor). It was a very simple wedding. I think I paid $15 for my wedding dress. It was a white, floor-length formal. We bought flowers and a cake. We were going to have our wedding in the back yard of this pastor's home but of course it rained. So we were married in front of the fireplace in the living room. I still have a picture of my little bouquet draped over a white Bible with streamers hanging down.

On one of the streamers, Zeral had attached a card that he had written to me on our wedding day. It read: To "D" From "Z" (and contained a few Bible verses). I had been so excited and so nervous that I didn't see the card until later when someone pointed it out to me.

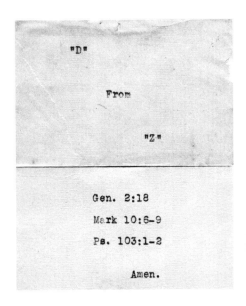

We didn't really get a portrait made of our wedding until six months later because the money just didn't quite reach that far. By the time we finally got our portrait, it was taken from the waist up, because I was six months' pregnant.

My sister, Ila was my bridesmaid and my husband chose a friend of his from school. My mother came up from St. James where she lived, along with my little brother and a sister-in-law. Unfortunately, none of his family was able to attend the wedding because of the distance. You know . . . we were married for 53 years and yet in all that time, our parents—his parents and my parents—never once met. I always thought that was very unusual.

We rented a little cabin out by a lake for our honeymoon. The pastor/friend, in whose home we were married, took us to a hotel the night we were married. Then he picked us up the next day and took us out to the lake where we spent the week. At the end of the week, he and his wife came out and picked us up and took us back into town. That was our wedding and our honeymoon!

The summer after we were married, we worked at a camp just outside of Minneapolis. This camp had been started during the depression by some WPA workers right after World War I when things were really tough. All of the cabins were small teepees. There was a lodge and a big dining room and a kitchen. We each got a job out there. My husband was singing in a quartet at that time and so each member of the quartet also got a job at the camp, so they could practice during the summertime. My husband worked in the bakery and he learned to bake bread from an elderly man who was baking bread for the camp. And I worked in the kitchen. People at the camp, who didn't know that we were married, thought Zeral and I were just 14 or 15 year olds because we looked so young. And I heard criticism, "why is that little 15-year old girl spending so much time with that boy in the bakery." And even though I had a ring on my finger to prove that I was married, nobody seemed to pay much attention to that. I had to show it many times in order to prove that I was married.

When summer was over, we went back for our third year of Bible school. I was pregnant by December. I dropped out of school the spring semester and Joanna Jean was born on August 19, 1944. Three months later,

I was pregnant again. Zeral graduated in the spring of 1944 and then went on to attend seminary and Spanish classes.

Although I still lacked a year to graduate from Bible School, Zeral suggested that I take a missionary medical course offered by the school. We knew it would better prepare us for the mission field.

We lived five minutes from the school in a one-room apartment and our classes coincided. We arranged to meet halfway, synchronizing our watches. The baby was only left alone for 2-1/2 minutes with the neighbor lady keeping watch through her open door. While I was gone, Zeral would bathe Joanna and give her the bottle. This arrangement worked well for that semester.

It was during our last year in Bible school that we were challenged by a speaker in our chapel to become missionaries. Paul Fleming said, "It was wrong for anyone to hear the gospel twice before everyone had heard it at least once." And so we took that phrase to heart. My husband was a very, very sincere young man and wanted so badly to do what God wanted him to do. In his written testimony of later years, Zeral explained how he had surrendered every part of his body to serve God:

We had a speaker at chapel (I think it was Dr. Walter Wilson) who said something like this: 'You must surrender to Jesus every part of your body—your eyes, your nose, mouth, stomach, liver, etc.' So I went back to my apartment and because I lived alone and had total privacy, I laid face down, flat on the floor, and tried to visualize myself at the foot of the cross where Jesus died. He was hanging there watching me and listening to my voice. So I said, 'Lord Jesus, I give you my hair, my head, my lips, mouth, tongue, teeth,' etc. On and on I went through every part of my body that I could name. And I gave them all to Jesus, to do His will and to serve Him. Of course, I have failed many times to live that total surrender, but I mean it now just as much, or more, than I did almost fifty years ago."

Quoted from the testimony of Zeral Brown

My husband, Zeral Louis Brown, was born in 1921, in the little town of Clarkston, Washington. He was the second child of the Brown family. The first child was also a boy, but he died at the age of one from meningitis. His name was Ezra, named after an uncle. So when the second son was born, they decided to change the first two letters of that name "Ez" to "Ze" and that's how they came up with the name "Zeral." His father's name was "John Brown" and they didn't like that name because of a song that had been popular some years before that said, "John Brown's body lays molding in the grave." They wanted to get as far away from the

25

name of "John" as possible. And, as Zeral would often say, "so they started with the letter 'Z' and they came up with the name Zeral."

Zeral never liked his name. He always wished that he had changed it in his earlier years to "Z. Louis Brown" and go by his middle name. But this didn't happen until he got to Cuba and he was advertised in the eastern end of the Island of Cuba for a city-wide campaign as "Zeral Louis Brown." A boat was blown up at a harbor and the Cubans of course blamed the "Yankees" for that, so the leaders of the church decided it was time to change his name. From then on he was known in Cuba as "Luis Castaño." When we moved from Cuba to Mexico, he continued to use this name.

Jehovah-Jireh

And my God will meet all your
needs according to his glorious
riches in Christ Jesus.

Philippians 4:19

We joined a mission headquartered in Fort
Wayne, Indiana and moved there while we waited for
our second child, Philip, born September 5, 1945. Zeral
was intent on going as a missionary to the country of
Sumatra, a jungle Island in the East Indies. He wanted
to go where no one else had gone and build on no other
man's foundation (according to Paul in Romans 15:20).
However, it was right after World War II and all
missionaries in that country had just been released from
Japanese concentration camps—that field was closed to
missionaries. We met a lady from Indiana who had been
held there. She weighed 60 some pounds and had
suffered terribly. The President of the mission we joined
(World Christian Crusade) suggested we consider going
to the Dominican Republic, since we had a very young

family and the country was more civilized. Zeral was disappointed, to say the least, but accepted his suggestion because he was anxious to be on the field.

We packed up our '35 Ford, took our babies, and started out to visit churches and individuals to raise our support. Philip was 8 weeks old and Joanna was 1 year and 8 weeks.

November is not a good month to travel the northern part of the States. We encountered our first blizzard as we headed for Minnesota and my home for Thanksgiving Day. Our car was a pre-war vehicle, which means we had good tires and well made machinery, but it was new to us. In the heart of the blizzard, we had a flat tire. At the same time, the heater went out. The spare tire was fastened on the back and covered over by a steel frame. Zeral didn't know how to remove the frame. Just before taking a hammer to beat it off, he found a keyhole that was operated with the ignition key. It wasn't long before the tire was changed and we were on our way to finding a mechanic to get our heater fixed. What made it more difficult was our baby had problems with his diet. Every time I gave him his bottle, he vomited it all over his clothes. I had to strip him completely in the cold car and find dry clothes to put on him.

We arrived at my home after midnight so thankful that mom had the house warm and was waiting up for us. We stayed with my parents on the farm until after Christmas. In the meantime, we saw a doctor and were told to strengthen the baby's formula and begin feeding him solid foods.

After Christmas, a reunion was scheduled for the Bible school quartet in St. Louis, and a meeting was scheduled in a church in Omaha, Nebraska. We again packed our car, putting the top part of a baby buggy in the back seat for the baby and made a bed on the other half of the seat for Joanna. It was the middle of winter in Minnesota and we were beginning our trip to the west coast, Zeral's home country. We stopped in Council Bluffs, Iowa to visit friends of my family. Zeral left me here with the children while he made the trip by car to St. Louis for the reunion. While in St. Louis, the four men each stayed in private homes. An offering was taken for them at the church where they sang and was divided among the guys. If I remember right, each one ended up with $50.00. This was the money that got us to Omaha and on to the West coast.

Zeral is on the left in the back row

The family where Zeral stayed asked him whether he had sufficient funds for the trip and he responded, "God will provide." So Mr. Elliott took out his credit card and gave it to Zeral and said, "Just sign my name and when you get there, and you have the money, just send me a check and return the card." This was the beginning of our life of faith. God became "Jehovah-Jireh"—the "God who provides." We kept all the receipts and upon arriving in Salem, Oregon, a lady we just met gave us a check for $100.00. All the receipts added up to that amount and we mailed the check and the card back to St. Louis. We experienced firsthand what Paul said in Philippians 4:19, "My God will meet all your needs according to his glorious riches in Christ Jesus."

In spite of the season, the mountains, and the miles, we had a memorable trip. Each night, we stayed in a motel. Zeral filled up with gas while we waited in a restaurant to be served (no fast foods). Then at the motel, we each bathed a baby and got a good night's sleep. By the way, these were the days of no disposable diapers or bottles. We warmed the bottle and the baby's food on the manifold as we traveled. We would stop after a few miles, grab the warm bottle and food, and be on our way.

One evening, as we were coming into Logan, Utah, it was dark. Zeral was sleepy and so he turned the wheel over to me. I had little experience driving, and of course the car was a standard shift. Immediately, we started down the mountains on hairpin curves. I was never so scared! But, we made it to the next town, safe and sound.

At this time, Zeral's parents were living in northern Washington for the apple-picking season. His sister and her husband were also there. So we headed up north to see them. How great it was to be with family! We stayed only a few days and then headed back down to Portland and Salem. Before we left, Zeral's dad gave us a twenty dollar bill, not knowing we were down to our last penny.

In Portland, we were invited to visit a church of an old friend of Zeral's. In fact, Delores was instrumental in influencing him in his early Christian life. Delores was a widow with one child, who lived with her sister and brother-in-law in a lovely home in Portland. We got a motel in Portland and then went to their house for dinner. I will never forget arriving with my two babies to find the table set for all four of us, with tall goblets, lots of silverware, and no high chairs. Later when we arrived at the church where Zeral was to speak, there was no nursery. Needless to say, after church I went back to the motel and told Zeral that I could not continue doing this with babies to care for. I asked him to take me to his sister's house in Bremerton, Washington, and leave me there while he proceeded to visit churches and individuals.

Zeral finally found housing for us in Salem, which was his hometown. He had gone through all the grades of school there and had many friends. First Baptist Church family took us under their wings and made us feel at home. One day I got a phone call from the pastor, Lloyd Anderson. He wanted to speak with Zeral but he wasn't at home, so he asked me what we were doing in Salem. I bluntly told him that we were looking for people to partnership with us so we could leave for the mission field. When he asked me how much promised monthly support we needed, I told him $225.00. He thanked me and hung up the phone. He later called Zeral into his office and told him the church wanted to back us for the full amount. They planned a commissioning service for us. Soon we were on our way back to Indiana and the mission headquarters.

We drove straight through to Minnesota, stopping only for gas and food. I remember one time in the early hours of the morning when we decided to stop for a cup of coffee. We were so tired, we skipped the coffee and lay on each other's shoulders and went to sleep for a few minutes.

Back in Fort Wayne, we continued to prepare to leave for the field but lacked money for transportation and supplies, such as clothing and shoes for growing children for the next five years. Since I sew, I tried to buy fabric but this was a scarce item right after the war.

An unexpected trip to the hospital delayed us even more as Zeral had to have an appendectomy. In the meantime, we had missionary housing. Three families lived together in a home owned by the mission organization.

God worked miracles and money came from unexpected sources to meet our needs. By May 1st, we were ready to leave. After saying goodbye to the mission family, we climbed into our car and were off to Florida and on to the Dominican Republic.

Upon arriving in the little town of El Seibo, we lived with the Jesups (another missionary family) and helped with the church they started there.

In our shipment, someone had given us an old, upright organ, the kind you pump with your feet. Zeral had had some music lessons when he was a kid and, being somewhat talented, he began to practice two new hymns each week. Then he played those hymns in the service that Sunday. He seldom took his fingers off the keys to cover his mistakes, so that we couldn't tell when a phrase began or when it ended. I brought this to Zeral's attention, telling him that it was difficult to sing along in this manner. He then made an effort to make the breaks more noticeable.

We handed out written invitations and advertised with a P.A. system, but only a few people attended. We rented a better location thinking that would help. After nine months of studying Spanish, Zeral preached his first sermon. I was given the job of teaching the little ones in Sunday school. I don't know if the children ever understood a word I said.

When we finally moved into our own home, I hired a girl to help me in the house and go to the market for our food. Having two small children, I couldn't take them with me, nor could I leave them alone. I didn't know enough Spanish yet to deal with the vendors. Everything was so primitive. We had no refrigeration so we had to buy food for one day at a time. Only two cuts of meat were available—with bone or without bone.

The cow was butchered and then hung up by its feet out in the open market, in all the heat and flies. We tried to buy as early as possible before the flies got it all. I do believe they killed the oxen when it was too old to pull an ox cart. Tough? I used a pressure cooker and for one pound of meat to be tender enough to eat, I had to cook it an hour. Sometimes it was all strings. There was no such thing as ground meat. Chickens were available, but only live ones, so we ate few. The only fresh vegetable that was available was cabbage. Needless to say, cabbage is my children's favorite food.

The girl we hired was not a Christian, so counting the change when she returned was a necessity. We soon began missing pieces of our silverware. We discovered that she would hide one piece at a time in an empty can and slip it into her pocket on her way home each evening. We had to let her go and hire a different girl to do the work.

The only cook stove we had was a charcoal burner. I thought I was really suffering, having to cook all my meals on charcoal. Then we went home on furlough and everyone had a charcoal grill in their backyard and considered it a lot of fun.

Our money was sent to us by mail once a month. On $225, we were often down to our last dime. Then sometimes, it didn't come at all. The mail system could not be trusted. On one occasion when we had not received our check, we took our last penny and sent a telegram to the mission office in the states. They sent a telegram back to us saying, "Check at the post office for it." We just looked at each other and wondered, "Where do they think we get our mail? Do they think we have mail carriers in these remote villages?"

At the time we lived in the Dominican Republic, Rafaél Leonidas Trujillo was the ruthless dictator of that country. He ruled with an iron hand. Because of reprisals and ever-present spies, we were fearful to ever mention his name even in private conversation. Either we made the letter "T" with our fingers or we substituted the name "Mr. Smith." Zeral taught English in the public high school and was aware of the presence of his henchmen even there. Word got around of people disappearing after making derogatory remarks about Trujillo. Every house had his picture on the wall to demonstrate loyalty. Even our children were affected. Upon arriving in Miami, as we began our furlough after 5 years of service, our son of 7 years could not repeat the name of Trujillo but called him "that President."

For God so loved the world . . .

Amazing Grace, how sweet the
sound, That saved a wretch like me.
I once was lost but now am found,
Was blind, but now I see.

Excerpt from Lyrics
by John Newton (1725-1807)

After one year, we felt ready to begin our own work in another town and God led us to the village of Hato Mayor. We rented a house big enough for our family and room to begin holding services. While we prepared the corner room for a chapel, we continued to practice our Spanish. Our landlord was a Puerto Rican with ill-fitting false teeth. Zeral thought that if he could learn to understand him—he could understand anyone. Nito loved to visit. He often took us to his place in the country for day outings. Our favorite pastime was to climb in his mango trees and eat mangos by the dozen, peeling them with our teeth.

Our main job was to furnish the chapel, which meant making benches, a platform and a pulpit. Money was scarce so we decided to ask the Lord for funds to buy lumber. Each day we visited the post office to see if a letter had come with a check. When we received $5, we got into our little '35 Ford and went to Santo Domingo, a trip of about three hours each way over graveled roads. We bought enough lumber to make one bench, along with nails, screws, sandpaper and varnish. While making our bench, we prayed for enough money to buy more lumber. Sometimes we received a check for $10, so we could buy enough supplies for two benches. Zeral's dad came to visit and made a railing around the platform. A friend sent fabric to make a curtain for the railing. We needed an organ. Two school teachers from Indiana bought us a little portable organ and shipped it to us. We needed a pulpit. The wooden box in which the organ was shipped was in good condition. Zeral turned the box inside-out, sanded and varnished it, and made a slanted shelf for his Bible and we had a pulpit.

After six months, we were ready to begin services in November of 1948. Because we expected opposition from the nationally recognized religion, we waited until the late afternoon to advertise the meeting. We prepared flyers to hand out from house to house and then used our P.A. system on the top of our car to announce the event. We asked the police if they would block off our street just outside our little chapel so we could hold an open-air meeting. Fellow missionaries were invited to participate. Grace Augsberger played the organ. Jack Cook preached. Marie Jesup and Zeral sang a duet. A borrowed flatbed served as a platform and our benches, along with added chairs, were put out into the street and the people came. We announced the opening of our chapel for services. This was held on a Sunday evening and our first service in the chapel was held the following Wednesday evening. At that very first meeting, four young men indicated their desire to receive Christ. I believe at least two of them were definitely born again. They began to attend services regularly. It wasn't long before one of them left to attend another church in town.

Alejandro Mota continued faithful and Zeral began at once to disciple him. Each night, Zeral took him with him when he went out to hold open-air meetings in the villages around Hato Mayor.

Alejandro was asked to give his testimony. He was a young man of about 21 years, who lived in the country and had no education beyond the third grade. He didn't know what a testimony was, so Zeral said,

"Just learn the verse John 3:16 and then say 'two weeks ago, I accepted Christ as my Savior'." Each night, Alejandro stood before the microphone and said, "One week ago, I accepted Jesus Christ as my Savior. The Bible says in John 3:16: 'For God so loved the world, that he gave his one and only Son that whoever believes in Him will not perish but have eternal live.'" And each week he would increase the number of days since he was saved. Thus began his training. Later we began a Bible Institute for him and a few other young people who had come to know our Savior. Alejandro went on to become a preacher, starting churches in other areas. In one of the villages where he preached, a little 8-year old boy named Rudy was saved, along with his mother. Jacinto "Rudy" De La Cruz continued faithful in the services, went on to finish high school and his studies at the Bible Institute. He is a university graduate and now the Pastor of the Iglesia Bautista Quisqueyana, one of the largest and fastest-growing churches in Santo Domingo.

On one of his trips to a distant village, Zeral heard about a Christian woman and her mother living up on a mountain. When they arrived in the village, Alejandro and a couple of the other young men carried the portable organ on their shoulders up the mountain to her home. Zeral played the organ and they all sang hymns and Zeral gave the message. The lady invited Zeral to come out to a little hut behind her house to meet her elderly mother. Her mother, who was blind, lived in a dirt-floored hut that you couldn't even stand in. The only way she was able to get around the hut was to crawl on her knees. Zeral led this woman to the Lord.

We saw her years later in the city of Santo Domingo and were told that she had remained faithful to God all those years. Isn't it wonderful that God's love reaches even to a little hut in the mountains of a distant village?

No village is too far for God.

We started a Children's Service on Tuesday evenings. With my very limited Spanish, I was put in charge and presented the Bible story each week often using colored slides to illustrate the story. Grace Augsberger played the organ and helped with the music. However, she knew less of the language than I did. One night I was telling the story of David and Goliath. I couldn't remember whether "giant" was pronounced "he-gan-te" or "ge-han-te," so I interchanged the word and half of the time I said it one way, and the other half of the time I said it the other way. In spite of my handicap, the children came.

The people of the town of Hato Mayor were entirely different from those of El Seibo. After five years of ministry in El Seibo, only one person had come to know Christ. When it was decided to close the work and move our missionaries out, only one person came to say "goodbye" and he only wanted to know if the house would be for rent.

In Hato Mayor, the people were open to the gospel and came to the services, in spite of opposition by the established religion. Sometimes they had to hide their Bibles as they came through the center of town but they came. One by one, individuals came to know the Savior.

Superstitions, Tarantulas, and a Stoning

Those who know your name will trust in you, for you, LORD, have never forsaken those who seek you.

Psalm 9:10

I became pregnant with our third child in 1949. Philip began to pray for a brother and Joanna prayed for a little sister. We always said that God answered both of their prayers—Sharon turned out to be all girl on the outside but had the makings of a boy on the inside.

I learned a lot about the culture and superstitions during that time, especially after Sharon was born. On our first visit to a doctor in Santo Domingo, he prescribed Vitamin B shots because he said that almost all American women were anemic. We were sent back to our village with three bottles of medicine, each containing enough for 10 injections. The local drug store sold us the hypodermic syringe and needle. Zeral proceeded to inject one shot into my hip each night. For having no prior experience, he did a good job, but . . .

ohhh . . . they were so painful. I think the needle was made for an animal, it was so large. I stood the pain each night for 29 shots and then said, "No more!" However, I do believe that I felt better than I had since my previous child was born four years earlier.

While pregnant with Sharon, I began to have problems with an itchy head. I washed my hair often but couldn't seem to relieve the itch. I finally asked the girl who worked for us to check my head because it felt like something was crawling on my scalp. She laughed at me and said, "anyone who washes their hair so often can't have such problems!" But sure enough she found I had a good head of lice crawling around. I discovered that my daughter, Joanna was using my comb and brush on her little friends in the street. I checked her head and found that she too had the same problem. I had never come up against such a problem and didn't really know what to do about it. The only poison we had on hand was the old fashioned DDT crystals, which we used in our garden. We mixed some of the crystals with some kerosene and using the outdated hand sprayer, Zeral sprayed my head while I protected my face with a towel. It stung a little but after one more application we saw no more evidence of lice. I then gave Joanna the same treatment with similar results. This occurred just before I went to the clinic to have my baby.

The doctor we went to had a two-room clinic and a delivery room on the second floor of a downtown building. When I began to have contractions, we quickly made the trip to the capital. However, after the doctor examined me, he decided I wasn't ready to deliver yet. He tried bringing on the contractions with quinine but with no effect. So I returned to Hato Mayor and waited another month. The second time we made the trip to the city, I asked if I could stay at the clinic until the birth because the wait so far from the city was too nerve-racking. We arrived in the morning and Zeral returned home immediately. That very same evening, I leaned forward in my chair, my water broke, and the contractions began in earnest. I sent word with a friend to call Zeral to let him know to return at once. Unfortunately, there was only one telephone in the town so by the time he got the message, loaded his car with friends, and made the three-hour trip back to the city, our Sharon was already born. I was so disappointed that he couldn't stay and at least be with me for awhile, but he had to take his carload of people back home. The next day, the baby got the hiccups after taking a bottle. So the nurse showed me how to stop the hiccups. She had never heard of burping a baby. She took a little string from the baby's clothes and wet it with her spit, rolled it up and put it on the baby's forehead. This was my first experience with Dominican superstitions.

According to another superstition, because it was cloudy and rainy outside, all the windows had to be closed so that the baby's stool wouldn't turn green. Three days later, I was in a taxi on my way back to Hato Mayor and ate an apple. Everyone thought I was going to die for sure. Apparently, after giving birth, women are supposed to stay indoors for 40 days. And they don't dare wash their hair, or put their hands in flour, eat fresh fruit, wear heels, or drive a car. I broke all the rules.

Very soon after Sharon was born, I thought that I was pregnant again. Needless to say, this was very disappointing. I remember so well the day I left all my daily work and went out to spend the day with the children. I decided that if God wanted me to have a large family then I would do it well.

We had our share of insects and animals in the DR. While living in our home in El Seibo, each morning we noticed feces of some kind of animal on the floor of

51

our dining room. It was too small to be a cat, but too large to be an insect or lizard. One morning around 2:00 or 3:00 a.m., we were both awakened by a 'plop, plop, plop' sound. Zeral grabbed his flashlight and ran out of the bedroom to see what was making that noise. What he found was a large toad, bigger than two men's fists put together. We discovered this toad lived under the walls of our shower. Since there was no drain in the floor, all the water from the shower ran out under the wall, down an open cement drain, along the back of our house, then down the side and across the front of the house. The drain beside the house was shared by the neighbors and, unfortunately, they used it for a bathroom. When the sun shone on the open drain (filled with urine), the odor would enter our bedroom windows just above the drain. We endured this for over a year.

Huge roaches lived in our outhouse. We bought insect spray, DDT, and anything else we could find. However, it seemed that it only chased them to the neighbors' side of the building until the stuff lost its strength and then they were back again.

Our house in Hato Mayor had wooden floors, walls and a ceiling. Every morning we noticed a pile of bird dirt on the dining room floor and had no idea where it was coming from. We would clean it up and the next morning, it was there again. Finally, we looked up at the ceiling one night and saw a bat hanging from the knothole—so the mystery was solved.

One night after the city had just shut down the generator and we were all tucked in our beds, our son (age 2 or 3) yelled out to his dad, "There is a tarantula in my bed!" We quickly lit the flashlight and ran into the next bedroom where our two children were sleeping. A large centipede (about 6-8 inches long and an inch wide) crawled out from under Philip's mosquito net. It had just crawled across his leg. We quickly ran for the broom and chased it into the bathroom next door and killed it. Centipedes like that are poisonous and can make a person very sick, but fortunately their bite is not fatal.

After we bought property outside of town, we battled tarantulas—especially in the outhouse. Our daughter, Joanna, got into the habit of taking a stick and a flashlight to the outhouse at night. She would bang the stick around the inside of the hole to scare any tarantulas away before sitting down. We used this outhouse until we could finish the bathrooms in the house.

Our doors of the house in Hato Mayor were very tall and cut in half from top to bottom. There were no windows in the house so we were either in the dark or we left the doors open for light. The problem was, the chickens, dogs, cats, and kids went in and out at will. We cut the doors in half the other way so that we could open the top part for a window and keep the bottom half closed.

We liked sitting in the living room as a family at night. Unfortunately, the roaches and flying ants also liked the light. They would fly in and hit the wall behind us and drop down to the floor. Zeral loved to practice his organ in the evenings. The children in the street heard the music and were very curious how Americans lived. Soon the doorway was filled with little, black faces. I felt like a monkey in the zoo.

It was Christmas Eve. All three missionary families and their children were enjoying a time of fellowship when suddenly the Jesup's three-year-old son, Jimmie, began vomiting. His mother had taken him to the local doctor earlier that week because of a serious case of diarrhea, with no results. Since he was becoming dehydrated, the Jesups immediately climbed into their

Jeep station wagon and left for the hospital in Santo Domingo, a three-hour trip over gravel roads. The rest of us began to pray. The next morning the Jesup's oldest son, who was five years old, began having the same symptoms. We only had two vehicles between the three families. Zeral and I took the remaining vehicle (a Jeep pickup truck) and rushed Rickie to the hospital, leaving our three children with the Augsberger family. Upon arriving at the hospital, we found the first child under an oxygen tent with a fever of over 105. Lyle and Marie Jesup were very distraught, thinking they were going to lose him. It was difficult to tell them that we had just brought in their second son.

The next day we got a telephone call from Hato Mayor telling us that our little Sharon (who was only a year and a half old) was beginning to show similar symptoms. But the remaining family had no vehicle. Because the Jeep truck had only one seat, Zeral jumped into the truck and drove back to Hato Mayor, picked up our baby and returned to the hospital (a 5-6 hour round trip). This time, Ivan Augsberger came back to the hospital with Zeral, in order to take the vehicle back. Little Sharon was put into a crib with a hypodermic needle in the muscle of her upper leg to feed her fluids and keep her from dehydrating. Her little leg swelled up twice its size as she attempted to crawl around the crib. A day or two later, Ivan arrived at the hospital with his oldest son, who was coming down with the same illness. By New Year's Eve, we had four of our seven children in the hospital. The illness was diagnosed as a lighter form of Cholera. Praise to God that all the children survived and we were able to return to our homes.

During this time we became aware of changes in our mission. We could not agree with the doctrines brought in by the new Director. Zeral decided that it was necessary to resign. Our fellow missionaries, who were on furlough at the time, also resigned and joined another mission board. They encouraged us to do the same. In order to do this, Zeral (at least) had to return to the states. He was to be gone for three months so he could visit our sponsors and let them know about the changes. I'll never forget the morning he left. The three children and I were standing on the front porch crying as we waved goodbye. Sharon was 10 months old. Three months alone in a foreign country caring for three children was not fun.

I love to read but remember promising myself during this time that I would never pick up a book while the children were awake. Thus, in the afternoon during their naps and at night, I read every book I could get my hands on. I read books that I wouldn't normally even take a second look at—like a biography of Benjamin Franklin and a book about Italian Sculptures. These books were part of a set of classical books loaned to me by our fellow missionaries.

Since talking by telephone was not an option, we relied on letters to keep in contact. Zeral asked me to make a list of things that I wanted him to bring from the states. I got out the Sears catalog and made up a list, mostly clothes, shoes, fabric to cover a sofa, books, chairs, a few dishes, and so forth. Zeral wrote to me after three months and asked permission to stay another month to fulfill other requests for meetings. He knew I wouldn't like it, so he added, "Just think of all the lovely things I am bringing for you." My response was, "If you think I prefer things to having you home, you're crazy." He stayed the extra month anyway.

Zeral returned with enough money to buy a new Jeep pickup and a good size piece of land just outside of town. We decided to build a house for us and a building for the church. The men divided the work between the three families. Lyle Jesup was to do the preaching in the church in town and Ivan Augsberger was in charge of evangelism. By the time Zeral left for his trip home, he and Ivan were taking the gospel to hundreds of sugarcane villages and small towns all over that end of the Island. Finally, for lack of funds and because our little Ford just gave up, that ministry had to be stopped. With the new Jeep fixed up as a sound truck, they were now able to renew this effort. Zeral was put in charge of construction. Grace, who was a former school teacher and had two kids of her own, taught the six children who were of school age. Marie took charge of the women's work and I continued to hold classes for the Dominican children.

Our home was the first building to be built. A contractor shared a house plan that Zeral liked, so we built a four-bedroom house. It was in a lovely setting along a creek under a large tree, a good distance from the road. We moved as soon as it was finished enough to live in. Of course that meant no water, no inside bathrooms, and plain, unpainted walls with the two-by-fours sticking out. But we loved it! Moving out of our rental house in town meant that we could expand our meeting place by moving it into the dining and living rooms. By this time, we had more than crowded out our little chapel in the corner room. A Bible Institute was begun with each of the missionaries teaching a class.

Our children loved living in the country. Philip loved playing with tools. He got hold of a post-hole digger (native-style), which consisted of a long handle with a sharp blade on the end. I asked Zeral if he didn't think it was a dangerous tool for a 5-year old but he didn't agree with me. Then one day we heard a scream from out in the yard and discovered the blade had landed on Phil's second toe and severed it almost completely: only a piece of skin held it to his foot. We wrapped it in a towel and rushed him to the hospital about an hour away. The doctor sewed the toe back on and put his leg in a cast, all the way to his knee—all except his toes. Zeral stayed with him the first day and then sent for me. Philip was hospitalized for a week. The toe did grow back on and he has had no problems with it.

Our new home just outside of town was on some acreage near a small creek. Often cows would wander in the yard and the neighbor's chickens loved to bring their chicks into our yard. One hen decided she wanted to lay her eggs on our couch. One chore that the children had was to chase the cows and chickens out of the yard.

When I took the children home to my family's farm in Minnesota, they soon felt the need to chase the chickens off the place. They also noticed steers in a pen near the barn. Philip was soon found inside the pen trying to get rid of the cows. When he was told not to do this because the steers could turn on him and hurt him, he told us not to worry; they would just jump right over the fence. My family was not sure what to think of these little "foreign" kids.

While living in Hato Mayor, the four missionary men decided they needed to invade the city of Higüey with the gospel. Higüey is the religious center in the Dominican and the people there were very fanatical about their religion.

On certain days, people made religious pilgrimages to that city to pay homage to their saint. Many people would make promises to get healing or miracles or to solve their problems. When we lived on our property outside of town, we would witness these groups of people passing by on the road, making their way on foot to keep their promise. Usually they carried a box with a lighted candle in front of a picture of their saint. Often they would chant or sing as they went.

The guys had visited this city at times and handed out salvation tracts. Always people, mostly boys, would follow them down the streets yelling, "Evangelicos" or "Hallelujas."

Much prayer went into the possibility of taking the gospel there by means of an open-air meeting. So one day, all four of the missionaries, Zeral, Ivan Augsberger, Lyle Jesup, and Jack Cook, piled into Jack's open Jeep and they were on their way. They took the sound system, electric generator, Bibles, tracts, microphones, and large bell-type speakers. They parked in front of the cathedral near the park and began to play hymns over the speakers. They also announced over the microphones that they were going to hold an evangelical meeting and invited everyone to attend. At the same time, the priest turned on the cathedral's sound system and began to call all the people together to run those "evangelicals" out of town. And the people came—hundreds of them. These fanatics began to shout, make noise of every kind, and even took sticks and ran them over the corrugated metal fence in order to drown out the music and voices of the missionaries. Since this didn't seem to stop the men, the people soon began to throw stones and finally got hold of the Jeep and began to rock it. Zeral decided it was best to face the enemy and so he stood on the side of the Jeep. He quickly received a rock in his forehead. Finally when even the police could do nothing, they started up the Jeep and left town. Zeral's head was bleeding profusely so they stopped at each home to let us wives know what had happened and then went on to the hospital. It took the entire night to get a doctor to attend to his forehead. He arrived home the next day around noon with stitches and a bandage but fortunately no concussion.

All four of the guys were called to appear in court. Somehow this incident had been reported, and since the dictator was for religious liberty, they were asked to testify who the priest was who had caused the riot. However, even though they knew who had instigated the event, the men decided (as Christians who wanted to be able to continue to preach the gospel) that they would not name names. In later years, we were told that there are dozens of evangelical churches in that town. TIME Ministries has built three or four chapels there for pastors, one of whom was saved in a church we started in a small sugarcane village near Hato Mayor.

Life is full of 'Goodbyes'

There are many plans in a person's mind, but it is the counsel of the LORD which will stand.

Proverbs 19:21

When our five years were up and it was time for our furlough, Zeral wasn't interested in returning to the states. I guess he felt that he had had his vacation. I felt differently and after some discussion, he suggested that I take the children and go alone. I agreed that I would . . . but he need not expect me to return. No more discussion. From then on we began to plan our year in the states. By planning, I mean that Zeral hired two girls to come in and type up letters to all the churches in the directories of the IFCA churches, independent Baptist churches, conservative Baptist churches and any others he could get his hands on. He told them that we were missionaries to the Dominican Republic, we had a 16-millimeter film of our work, we were going home on furlough and that we were available for a missionary conference, church service, Bible study, women's meeting, or whatever. We included a return-address post card with a place to check if they could use us. Before we left the DR, we had scheduled meetings for months into our vacation from one end of the country to the other.

Our travels led us all the way to the west coast and back as far as New York State. It was 16 months before we returned to the Dominican Republic. God provided us with a new car and a house trailer through a lady in St. Louis, who had given us a large gift toward our Jeep and our property. Having traveled with two small babies and stayed at homes of friends along the way before leaving for the mission field, we were so pleased that this time we would have our own home and be able to sleep in our beds each night. The two oldest children, now 6 and 7 years old, did not like traveling. Each place we stopped, they made new friends and then had to leave them. Grandma and Grandpa Brown invited the kids to stay with them and told us that they would put them in school in Seattle, Washington. We put Joanna and Philip on a plane in Chicago and, after changing planes in Minneapolis, they landed safely and spent the next nine months with their grandparents. In the meantime, we continued on our itinerary making our way to the west coast. Sharon, then almost 3 years old, stayed with us. She was a good traveler but missed her brother and sister. From then on, whenever I left to run any errand, she would cry until I returned. While in Salem we visited the children as often as possible and were able to spend Christmas with them. By March we were on our way back east, leaving the children with Zeral's parents once again. When school was out, Joanna and Philip flew back to Chicago where we picked them up. All of us were back in the DR by September.

While home in the states during a missionary conference in Pennsylvania just outside of Philadelphia, I received word that my mother had passed away. I left Sharon with Zeral and flew back to Minnesota to the funeral. She had just had gall bladder surgery and on the drive home from the hospital, suffered a heart attack from a dislodged blood clot. After the funeral, I flew back to Philadelphia.

Upon returning to the Dominican Republic, we felt that the ministry in Hato Mayor was in good hands with other missionaries and national pastors. We were led to begin a church in Santo Domingo. Before we had left on furlough, a building was constructed on the front corner of the new property, which served as a meeting place for the church and classroom for the Bible Institute.

We found a house for rent and moved into the capital city. The children were enrolled in an English-speaking school. Since several families from our church in Hato Mayor had already moved to Santo Domingo, we immediately started services for them in our home. This small group began to grow and it wasn't long before we were able to rent the front part of a house for our services. This house was owned by a lady involved in spiritism, who was very troubled. One day we went to open the doors for a service and found our benches, pulpit and organ in the street. We soon found a store building with a large open area, made more benches, and the work grew even more. Within two years, we had a group of 75 young people and many of them wanted to attend our Bible Institute.

At home, Zeral began piano and music lessons for Joanna and Philip. When school was out, we continued classes for the children to keep them busy. Zeral also taught Phil shop, while I taught sewing and cooking to Joanna. We both helped them with academic courses, especially reading and typing.

Our only car was our Jeep pickup. We had to drive several miles back and forth between the school and our house each day. We would take them to school each morning, pick them up at noon, return them to the school at 2:00 pm, and then pick them up in the afternoon. Traffic wasn't then what it is now, and to see a woman driving was very unusual. We always had to pass a police station on the way and there would be guards out in the street. Without fail, even though I tried to act very confident and dignified, I would go over a bump in the street just as I was passing the guards. If you have ever ridden in a Jeep truck, you know how humbling it is to be bounced almost out of control.

Zeral and I always worked together very closely. Since Zeral had so many talents and did so many things well, it made me feel more inferior and of less worth. I never learned to sing or play the piano or speak in public. I found it hard to meet new people or even express myself in a letter. I do remember the day that I decided my job was to be a good wife, keep the house clean, take good care of the children, have meals ready and on-time so that Zeral would be free to do what he did best—to go out and do ministry. I helped with the office work, such as typing up his letters, folding, stuffing, and mimeographing. There were no computers or printers in those days. He dreamed, created and planned, and I did the grunt work.

I never found it hard to follow God's will for my life. The hardest part was knowing what His will was. Just because someone suggested that I do something didn't mean that it was God speaking to me. My favorite verse is, and has always been, Philippians 4:6-7: "Be anxious for nothing, but in everything, by prayer and supplication, with thanksgiving, let your requests be made known unto God. And the peace of God will keep your hearts and minds in Christ Jesus." Another verse that always came to mind was 1 Thessalonians 5:18, "In everything give thanks, for this is the will of God in Christ Jesus, concerning you."

A short time after returning to the DR, Zeral received word that his father suffered a heart attack and died instantly. Because of lack of funds and the distance, he was unable to attend the funeral. Later that year, Zeral's mom came to visit us. She stayed a full year and was a great help to me. The hardest thing for her was the language barrier. She loved to visit but was unable to communicate in Spanish. Sometimes this made her angry because she thought people were talking about her. She was a wonderful mother-in-law and the children loved her. Together, we made all of Joanna's and Sharon's dresses.

As often happens in mission work, problems arose among the missionaries. Part of it stemmed from jealousy and part from inappropriate behavior on the part of one of the missionary wives. Zeral began to feel uncomfortable working in that atmosphere and gradually felt led to leave the country to serve as an evangelist to Spanish-speaking churches everywhere. I was very resistant to the idea, always finding it hard to adjust to changes. I begged him to stay, to find a way to solve the problem or work alone, but to no avail. Finally one night, during a rainstorm, we went to open the doors of the church for a Wednesday night service. As we sat in our Jeep pickup outside of the church, waiting for the rain to stop, I gave in and agreed to leave the country. Zeral had been agonizing for weeks over this decision. When I finally gave in, the relief in Zeral was so evident, as his spirit lifted. It was as if he could finally see a light at the end of a long, dark tunnel. We immediately began to make plans to leave even though it was six months before we finally said our goodbyes. We waited until the mission board could find a replacement.

We put an ad in the paper stating that an American couple was leaving the country and wanted to sell their household possessions. Wow! The people came in droves and paid well for everything that we had for sale. Our furniture that we brought down from the states was all old and well used. All of it was given to us while home on furlough, but it was American and valuable for that reason. A few pieces Zeral had made from used lumber. We were able to sell everything for a fantastic price and left the country with thousands of dollars.

We left the country with one suitcase full of clothes for all five of us, a trunk full of books, a mimeograph and a few heavy items of equipment. The money served to buy us our clothes and to make a down payment on a house in Boca Raton, Florida.

One of the last times of fellowship spent with the other missionaries was at Thanksgiving. We were invited to dinner at Ivan and Grace Augsberger's at their home in La Romana. Since "dinner" usually meant about 12:00 noon, we planned our arrival for about

11:30, just to make sure we would be on time. To our surprise, we entered the backyard on our way to the house and there was the turkey running around, very much alive! Not long after, their yard boy came up with a long machete in his hand and "whoop"—off went the turkey's head. Then began the work of dressing the animal, cleaning, gutting, and de-feathering it, before it was ready to bake. Grace didn't have a roaster and so, as a good missionary, she improvised and used an enamel covered tin bread box. After about an hour, we began to smell the odor of burned paint. The enamel was turning brown and overpowered any smell of roasted turkey. Dinner was served late in the afternoon with only one side dish, fried platano. The turkey was burned on the outside and not quite done on the inside. It was a very memorable Thanksgiving, to say the least.

A month or so before we left the Dominican Republic in 1956, a cruise ship arrived from Boca Raton, Florida. We all went down to meet the retired Christians from Boca Raton Bible Conference grounds, later called Bible Town. The director, Ira Eshelman, and his wife, invited us on the ship. They also invited us to visit them in Boca Raton, assuring us that we would have a place to stay.

Before leaving the Dominican, we made a visit to the church we started in Hato Mayor in 1948 to say goodbye to all our dear brothers and sisters there. The Genao family, one of the Dominican families in the church, invited us and the entire church family to their home for a farewell celebration. We have stayed in touch with this family all these years and, to this day, the Genao's daughter works with the children's ministry in the Santo Domingo church. And their granddaughter works with the children who are sponsored through the Samuel's Fund ministry that I started several years ago.

The first thing we did after we flew to Miami was go shopping for new clothes. Zeral planned to fly to Cuba to investigate the possibility of doing evangelistic work in the churches there. He first made arrangements for me and the children to catch a ride to Chicago with a young man from Costa Rica. My sister who was home on furlough from Morocco met us in Chicago at my aunt's house. And we saw television for the first time there. Then we boarded a train for my home in St. James, Minnesota. Because it was cold and we had lived in the tropics for so long, my sister supplied us with wool clothes. But the train was overheated and stuffy and we soon began to itch from the wool. That was the longest ride! And the children never wanted to ride on a train again.

While Zeral was in Miami and Cuba, I wrote the following letter to him from my home in St. James:

> I just got your letter and, therefore, we have had little time to think and less time to pray about living in Miami. I do wish we could talk things over before we make any decisions, so my advice would be to come north and let's spend a couple of weeks together here, talking and praying about it. But, don't forget a car. Why don't you investigate houses for rent before you come? Find out if they are available, how much they rent for, and if you find something, use your own judgment about renting it. I'd hate to land back in Miami with no place to go again. This is all I can say now, except you ought to know your wife by now, enough to know, she will go where you want her to go. I'm getting pretty lonely. Life is very different here. Phil and the girls love the farm and want you to buy a farm if we live in Miami.

> Love, Dorretta

After his visit to Cuba, Zeral flew to Detroit where he bought a used car and met us in St. James. After much prayer and discussion, it was decided that we would return to Florida. We accepted the Eshelmans' invitation to stay at the Bible Conference grounds in

Boca Raton. During our visit, we looked for a house in an area close to an airport, so that Zeral could make frequent trips to Spanish-speaking countries. My only request was that I could stay with the children and put them in school. God led us to a house in Boca Raton after weeks of looking in Miami, Ft. Lauderdale, and all of that area. We were really babes when it came to purchasing a house. The ads in the papers would say "stucco, bath and a half" and so forth. Zeral would walk up to strangers in a restaurant and ask, "What does this mean?"

The Boca Raton Bible Conference grounds provided a great place for fellowship. A regular church was formed and we became involved in it. I taught Sunday school and became President of the women's missionary meetings. When he was home, Zeral sang in the choir and sang some solo numbers.

Cuba and Castro

*Whatever town or village you enter, search
for some worthy person there and stay at his
house until you leave. As you enter the
home, give it your greeting. . . . If anyone
will not welcome you or listen to your
words, shake the dust off your feet when you
leave that home or town. I tell you the truth,
it will be more bearable for Sodom and
Gomorrah on the day of judgment than for
that town.*

Matthew 10:11-15

Zeral began to make regular trips into Cuba.
Because our support level dropped, he took a job as a
carpenter and worked between trips. They were
constantly building motels and private homes at the
conference grounds. More and more people wanted to
live there year round or attend the conferences held there
in the winter months.

We loaded up the children when school was out
and all went to Cuba. We took a large tent and set it up
in different places to hold services. We had taught the
children to play instruments and sing. Phil played the
coronet, Joanna played the violin, and Sharon played tap

77

bells. They all sang special numbers with their father and with one another.

Accommodations varied as we went from one place to another. Sometimes we were put up in private homes and sometimes in empty houses. Our main meal of the day was generally furnished by the people of the church who invited us to their homes. But we always fixed our own breakfasts and lunches.

Zeral took an old wardrobe trunk and fixed it to stand upright, built shelves in it for dishes and groceries and that, along with a camp stove, served us well. We always traveled with camp cots and mosquito nets. I have pictures of Joanna washing her hair in a rain spout. We always tried to make these trips fun for the children.

We often found horses to ride and went to tourist attractions or amusement parks.

When the children got older—Joanna was ready for high school and Phil was a year younger—we looked for a boarding school for them. We finally settled on Bob Jones' Academy in South Carolina. Then we took Sharon with us and traveled full-time in Cuba, teaching her on the road.

On one of our first trips to Cuba we were invited to a very small church in the country. We had bought a Volkswagen van and carried all of our equipment in it. Our equipment consisted of cots, mosquito nets, camp stove, wardrobe trunk (which was our kitchen), a portable organ, large lighted easel for my Bible stories, and our personal items. The church was off the main road at least a half mile. It was in disrepair and in need of a new roof. A large mound of dirt from ant hills covered the floor and a large hole in the roof did little to keep out the rain . . . and rain it did! We set up our beds and nets in a room off the main room, which was protected from the weather. Then Zeral left to go into a nearby town to get food supplies. There was no electricity, so when night came we lit a lantern. Sharon and I read books and waited until late for dad to return and finally went to bed. We watched the rats run around on the rafters. Sometime after we had fallen asleep, Zeral returned, having had to walk from the road in the rain, carrying the groceries in paper bags. He said it was raining so hard, he felt the water running down his legs. Upon arriving at the church, he lit the lantern and found that the eggs had broken and it was egg yolks—not water—that he had felt running down his legs. In spite of the rain, we cleaned up the church and had the roof repaired. We began holding nightly meetings and invited the people of that community. Many people came. One young man played the guitar every night and sang—sometimes a solo and sometimes a duet. Sometimes a group of young people would sing. But always, they sang the same song. It didn't matter to them that the guitar was lacking one string and was out of tune.

Sometime during that week we were able to bring our vehicle up close to the church. But, when it came time to leave to go to the next church, we had to get oxen to pull the car out of the mud back to the road.

For 62 nights we held meetings in different churches and towns and only missed two nights when Zeral begged off because of a stomach ache. Two of the young men visited many of our services at different locations and even came forward to accept Christ. One afternoon they came into the church where Zeral was studying and began to ask questions. Finally Zeral told them, "Listen, I know you are spies sent to find out why I, as an American, am here in Cuba. I am a missionary and I came here to preach the gospel and tell people how they can be saved and be sure of heaven. So you can return to whoever sent you and tell them this."

Zeral and Sharon provided the special music for our meetings. Sharon sang solos and duets with her father. I told a Bible story using black-lighted backgrounds and figures, which we purchased from an artist in Michigan. We got schoolbooks from the fourth grade teachers in Boca Raton and during the day I would teach Sharon her lessons.

So often in the more humble homes where we were given a place to stay, the shower room consisted of a little room with a cement floor and no furniture. We took a pail of water into the room and used a wash cloth and basin. After soaping ourselves, we used an empty tin can or cup to rinse off. The water ran out of the room and under the walls to the outside. In one place that we stayed, the outhouse doubled as the shower room. We heated the water on our camp stove, carried the water to the outhouse, and stood on slats built over the toilet hole to rinse off. But the hot water stirred up the fumes from below and made breathing a little difficult.

Only 90 miles separated the Island of Cuba from Key West. For $10.00, we could take the ferry over. As soon as Castro took over, the ferry was canceled.

By reading newspapers and listening to conversations, Zeral was convinced that the communists were infiltrating the government of Cuba and that it wouldn't be long before the door to the gospel would be closed. The revolution was building up and we could see tobacco barns burning along with sugarcane fields. Fighting was breaking out in some places and people were disappearing. Bearded soldiers were everywhere. Many missionaries were deceived and when Castro announced that he was a communist, they were completely disillusioned.

We sent the children back to South Carolina to Bob Jones' Academy in the fall of 1960. It was then we realized that to return to Cuba was inadvisable. We were getting reports of missionaries being refused re-entry into Cuba, after having all their equipment and possessions confiscated. It was reported that they had been exposing Castro's activities in the churches in Florida. Since we had also been telling everyone our opinion of the condition in Cuba, we decided not to return and risk losing everything.

TIME Ministries

We are therefore Christ's ambassadors,
as though God were making his appeal
through us. We implore you on Christ's
behalf: Be reconciled to God.

2 Corinthians 5:20

We decided to rent out our home in Boca Raton, buy a house trailer and car and move to the Mexican border. We had already made an exploratory trip in the spring to check out the possibility of ministering in the churches there.

The Rio Grande Bible Institute, outside of Edinburg, Texas, gave us permission to park our trailer on their property. This school taught Bible classes to Mexican students and also taught Spanish to Americans. I soon enrolled in the Spanish classes to perfect my language skills.

Zeral became busy holding evangelistic meetings in many of the Mexican churches on both sides of the border. Sharon and I would often accompany him on these meetings. We had enrolled Sharon in the public school and so returned home each night.

One of our first invitations to visit Mexico came from a former student of the Rio Grande Bible Institute. She invited us to visit her church in China, Nuevo Leon, Mexico. One of the families in her church invited us to dinner at their home. This was a very humble home with only a dirt floor and a thatched roof. The hospitality was unforgettable! They had killed their very young goat and prepared a delicious meal. However, being new to Mexico, we had much to learn. A platter of goat meat was set in the center of the table with the goat's head, eyes and all, laying on top . . . well prepared, of course. Our first course was a bowl of soup with mostly broth. Since we were given no silverware, we watched while our host picked up a tortilla, tore it in half and then in quarters, and began to scoop up the soup with the piece of tortilla. His fingers did not so much as touch the soup. So, ok . . . we would do the same. Needless to say, we had problems learning the technique and when we finished our hands were full of soup. Then came the main course, deliciously prepared goat meat. The goat meat was also eaten with tortillas as our only utensil. Being the honored guest, the head was given to me. I thanked them heartily and asked if I could take it home to eat it later, to which they agreed.

At the Bible Institute, we met a man who was dedicated to ministering to unreached Mexicans for Christ. He offered his converted beer truck if Zeral would go with him to find some of these villages. The day came for them to make their first exploratory trip. They had traveled only about 50 miles into the country when the truck broke down and they had to limp it back across the border. Not long after that they set another date and packed the truck with supplies and food. Once again they had only gone a short distance when a tire blew and they had to return home because there was no spare. A third trip was planned, but this time Zeral took our fairly new Dodge Dart. Believe it not, on a main road, a piece fell out from under the car and they ground to a stop. They limped home again without making contact. All this opposition was only taken as an attempt on the part of Satan to keep us from beginning a work in Mexico. While some people would have seen this opposition as God's way of closing the door to this area, these men persevered and successfully reached the village! We finally made contact with the village of

Pueblo Nuevo and began to make regular trips to hold open-air services.

We met a man living in this village whose aged mother was bedridden at the time. She decided to loan us a piece of property where we could put a chapel to hold services. Zeral began to put into action a plan for a portable chapel, which he had designed 18 years before in the Dominican Republic. Since most of the land in the country of the DR was owned by the large sugar industry and wasn't for sale, Zeral's idea was to build a portable chapel and place it on their property. If the sugar company objected, the chapel would then be taken down and moved. However, we left the Dominican Republic before this plan could be accomplished. Now in Mexico, we ran into a similar situation. All the land in these small villages was government-owned and could not be bought. So the solution was to build something portable that could be moved, if necessary.

We met a couple of young men (twin brothers) who offered to do the building. One of these young men had attended the Rio Grande Bible Institute and began to hold services in this little 12 x 24 chapel.

The first chapel design was to be in only four pieces, excluding the roof. Later, the design changed several times and became 4-foot panels with a corrugated tin roof in 4-foot widths. This design made it easier to handle during construction and also when moving the building.

During Christmas vacation in 1967, we received a phone call from a youth pastor of our acquaintance in Houston, Texas. He asked Zeral if he could bring his youth group down to Mexico and if we could give them a missionary experience. Zeral never turned down an opportunity and said, "Yes, we would be happy to do this." By this time we had bought the rights to use a small piece of property in the village of Pueblo Nuevo near our first chapel. There was only a small mud-brick house with a thatched roof and a hand-dug well. We quickly made a trip to Pueblo Nuevo to build an outhouse and a couple of shower stalls out of mud bricks. We had no time to put a roof or doors on the shower stalls, so we hung a blanket fastened to a long pole and placed it over the door openings.

What did we do for water? Well, believe it or not, we had "running" water: we filled a bucket by letting a pail down into the well, pulled it up and then ran to the shower stall (just like we learned to do in Cuba). We had to teach these young people how to soap up and then use a tin can of water to rinse. I'm sure they never forgot their experience!

My job was to feed these young people. We brought down most of our supplies from the states. Needless to say, our facilities were very primitive.

With very little advertisement, one group told another group, and soon our summer months and vacation times began to fill with groups of young people coming to experience missions firsthand. We devised a program of working in the morning and doing ministry in the afternoon and evening. This was the beginning of TIME Ministries. TIME is an acronym for The Institute of Missionary Evangelism. As requests came in for chapels, we had the young people building chapels in the mornings and then going into Monterrey to do ministry in the evenings. We would find a church or an open area (like a park) and go up and down the streets inviting people to services. We left a gospel track with each one we met. After the gospel services, we would return home late at night.

In the village of Pueblo Nuevo, we met a young man named Juan Davila. He had been saved in the little chapel and showed great interest in studying God's Word. He came frequently to ask questions about the

Bible. His pastor began to hold services in another village near Pueblo Nuevo called La Haciendita and would take Juan along with him. We soon had the young people build a chapel there and services were held once a week.

Excerpt from Juan Davila's testimony:

My name is Juan Davila Molina. I was born in an agricultural settlement by the name of Pueblo Nuevo in the state of Nuevo Leon, Mexico. I am the second son of a family of six children. I was born in a non-Christian home, and until the time I was 17 years old, I knew nothing about the Gospel. There was no one in the village who preached the Bible or who spoke to us about the Lord Jesus Christ, until our Brother Zeral Brown arrived in 1967. I was about 17 years old when Brother Brown came to our village. For us it was something new. Nevertheless, I did not accept the message of God at that time. I have an older brother who took much interest in the message and faithfully attended the services for a long time. I made fun of him. I was not interested in what he thought or what he believed about the Bible. . . . I would go to the chapel and sit with my friends in the street in order to criticize, judge, and make fun . . . . When I was 19, I went to the church out of curiosity. At that time, they were having special meetings with someone from outside Pueblo Nuevo who did the preaching. . . . The brother was speaking about salvation and judgment and how one could be saved. . . . The message of that night filled all my needs. For the first time in my life, I felt my need and gave my life completely to Christ. . . . My mother never liked the Gospel and still doesn't. My father tolerated anything and never talked to us about it. But my mother . . . thought this was just a passing thing, for she is a very strong Catholic. Then the time came for me to be baptized. I told her I wanted to be baptized. She became very angry and tried to prohibit my attending further services in the church. But since I was grown up, I could go out at night early without her knowing. I would go to the church. Then when the time arrived for baptism, I planned not to tell anyone in the family, much less my mother. I went to the baptism at the river. Later I arrived home with my clothes wet. When mother saw me, she was very angry. I told her then that I had decided to serve God and continue in His way in this church.

Zeral and I made regular trips into Pueblo Nuevo to encourage the pastor and to hold special evangelistic meetings. Often we showed movies or Bible slides to attract a crowd. Zeral would go to the village of La Haciendita and pick up all who wanted to attend these meetings.

The daughter of the family who loaned us the property on which to build the chapel in La Haciendita attended one night along with her father. We showed the film "Something to Die For" and Bertha accepted Christ.

Excerpt from Bertha's testimony:

I was born in a village of Mexico called La Haciendita. I lived with my parents and four sisters. We never attended a church of any kind. My mom taught us to worship saints and to ask miracles of them and also to go to healers for help when we were sick. These healers were called "curanderos." They had special rooms filled with pictures of saints (Saint Paul, Saint Peter, Saint Vincent and the Virgin of Guadalupe). When we went to him for help, he told us to pray to the saints in our house (there were pictures of saints) and ask them for a miracle. Then if we weren't healed, we were to go to his house. He would sweep us with fresh herbs and anoint us with oil and strike us on the face. We recited prayers to the saints. To enter his house, we had to take off our shoes. I heard the Gospel for the first time when I was 13 years old. Pastor Jose Ibanez came with Zeral Brown to my village to hold open-air services near my home on property belonging to my uncle. I liked the Gospel the first time I heard it. I liked the songs and the things they said. . . . When the invitation was given, I was drawn but didn't make a decision for fear of my family, especially my mother. My mother pretended to like the Gospel when the missionaries were present, but otherwise she was very much against it. One night when a car came to take many of us from La Haciendita to Pueblo Nuevo to see a special presentation of the film, "Something To Die For," I received Christ as my Savior. The thing that impressed me was the suffering and persecution of the young people in the film and how one girl said she would rather be "the dust of a diamond than a round stone." It was then I realized that I was a "round stone" that served for nothing, and I received Christ as my Savior. That night my problems began. All of my family turned against me except my father, who also was moved to accept Christ but was more fearful than I. They all became very angry because of my decision and constantly made fun of me. However, I knew that Christ was in me and would protect me, so was not unduly upset. . . . I asked permission of the pastor to teach a Sunday school class. Because I did something without asking my mother's permission first, she became very angry and beat me. Later she told me she could no longer handle me and that she was going to let me do as I pleased but that one day God would punish me. I continued to give classes to the children and received many beatings because of this. Each incident at home caused me to become more firm in my faith in Christ and in His Word. . . . At times I was encouraged to trust God, but at other times the threats and beatings from my mother were very real. . . . Two years passed and then the time came when I felt a desire to be baptized and dedicate my life completely to God. While waiting for this event, my father also was saved. He was moved to believe in

Christ as His Savior and became bold enough to make his decision known. That was a great blessing to me and helped me a great deal. The day we were to be baptized, there was a great problem in my house. The missionary, Zeral Brown, came the evening before to talk with me about being baptized. My father then spoke up and said he also was a believer and wanted to be baptized. My mother seemed agreeable and said it was up to us to do what we wanted to. The missionary left and then mother began to scold, berate, yell, and beat us (me more than my father). . . . God gave me courage along with my faith to follow the Lord in baptism no matter what. Even though I carried the marks and bruises of my beatings, I wanted to be baptized. . . . My mother continued to beat me, all the while saying I must deny Christ and give up my religion. I continued to say I just couldn't do that and she continued to beat me with a board and with the flat side of a machete. She pinched me, slapped me, pulled my hair, bit me and banged my head against the wall. I was bruised from head to toe. But nothing could get me to deny my Lord. . . . One of the young men who came to help the pastor in the services in the chapel on our property was Juan Davila. We became acquainted in these services but never had a chance to talk alone. One night some 10 months later while attending a service in Pueblo Nuevo, Juan spoke to me.

Due to much opposition from her mother, Juan and Bertha eloped but later returned to their families to be married again at home. After Juan and Bertha were married, we sent them to a Bible school outside the city of Monterrey.

Zeral was interested in using Juan to start a church in the Monterrey area, while he attended classes. We were led to rent a house in which to hold services and Juan began holding meetings there. This developed into the Elim Baptist Church and our present site in Monterrey for TIME Ministries. From this church, twelve other churches were planted in the surrounding areas and a Children's Home (Dulce Refugio, which means "Sweet Refuge") was built and opened.

Juan and Bertha Davila are the most outstanding workers that God has given us since we entered Mexico in 1967. Both are from small "ejidos" (agricultural settlements) far from the main highways. Who would have thought God would have had such precious jewels waiting for the Gospel light in such small, out-of-the-way and insignificant villages?

No village is too far for God to reach.

Besides conducting tours to Mexico in the summer, Zeral and I were invited to hold special meetings during the rest of the year. Near the end of the last tour one summer, Zeral was invited to speak to a youth camp by a church in Mexico City. The camp was located in the mountains. Even though it was 100 degrees weather in Monterrey at that time of year, it was cold in the mountains. The people of the church loaned us coats and mattresses. The church bus was loaded and up the mountain we went, higher and higher. It began to rain by the time we stopped near a stream. A campfire was started and we sat as close as possible to one another to keep warm, holding umbrellas over us to keep us dry.

It wasn't long before the young people, along with their adult sponsors, had erected two large tents—one for the gals and one for the guys. They laid the moldy, smelly, thin mattresses side by side. My bed was one of the mattresses laid on the ground and the Pastor's daughter slept next to me. Each night, she wet her bed and I woke to the strong smell of urine.

At the first meeting, we were told that the toilet facilities were two paths up the side of the hill: one path for girls in one direction and the other path for boys. The next morning, I met Zeral and we started up our different paths, but found that the rest of the group had gotten there first and hadn't waited to reach the holes.

So he and I decided to go off in a different direction to find a clean path.

I spent most of the time sitting by the fire trying to keep warm and dry. By the end of the third day when the camp was over, we had not even changed clothes or washed our faces. As soon as we arrived back in the city, we rented a motel room and took warm showers and welcomed the heated room.

Another time, Zeral and I were invited to participate in a conference in the town of Tampico. Workshops were planned and while Zeral taught Bible classes, I was to teach child evangelism classes to teachers. We were given a room in a private home. This home was situated alongside a highway where large trucks passed by day and night. The room was simply furnished with just a double bed with "no-sag" springs. However, the toilet facility was a little shack with a large log lying on the floor. The idea was to sit on the log and do one's duty. The most interesting part was there was no door on this building, just a curtain. And, every time a truck went by, the curtain was blown out so that one was completely exposed.

At another conference in Aztec Indian territory of Tamasunchale, we were treated to a nice hotel room in town. However, our meals were taken in a large building with the Indian congregation. The menu consisted of mostly beans and tortillas. Usually, one can count on at least the beans not being hot (picante) but not in this case. Everything was spicy hot! The last day of the conference, we took our meal in the hotel and ordered a large steak.

Bibleville

For we do not preach ourselves, but
Jesus Christ as Lord and ourselves as
your servants for Jesus' sake.

2 Corinthians 4:5

We continued to live on the Texas side of the border in order to keep Sharon in school. We bought a small house on two acres in South Texas in 1960. Joanna decided to leave Bob Jones University and continue her studies in the Pan American University in Edinburg, Texas, while living at home. She met John Berry that first year and was married in the summer of '64.

After Philip graduated from high school, he joined the Navy. When Phil finished his stint in the Navy, he enrolled in a Florida Bible college where he met his wife, Lori. They were married in 1970.

Sharon graduated from high school and then enrolled in a Bible college in Miami. There she met and married the dean of the school, Bruce Porter, in 1969. Bruce and Sharon planted a church in the Florida Keys.

Meanwhile, Zeral was asked to produce a radio program where he preached the gospel to all of Latin America. He offered Bible correspondence courses during this program. My job was to answer the letters from people who were interested and send out packets of information.

While living in the Rio Grande Valley, we became aware of thousands of northerners who spent their winters there, escaping the cold and snow of the north. Many of these retired people were Christians with many different skills, who were spending their winters playing cards or shuffleboard. Zeral was challenged to begin a Bible Conference in the valley with the purpose of harnessing all of their skills for missions.

In sharing this vision with others, an elderly man offered to give us a check for $10,000.00 to purchase property for such a venture. As we looked around for a good location, we located a two-acre piece of property on Morningside Road, north of Alamo, Texas. Other retirees were inspired to join us and helped put in a few trailer hook-ups, which we rented out for the winter months. Little by little, we were able to buy more property and put in more hook-ups. We began holding Bible conferences in the brick house located on the property.

Always, our main objective was to use these skilled retirees in promoting missions. While the men worked on improving the grounds, the women got together making quilts for the Mexican students, making rubber molds of gospel plaques in Spanish, and preparing the craft materials for the daily vacation Bible school classes in Mexico.

We took the retirees on frequent trips into Mexico to visit the people and see the ministry and the needs. By means of their generous offerings, we were able to build a large three-story building on the property we bought in Monterrey. We took them on work tours, during which they built bunk beds, repaired buildings, constructed a dormitory for girls, and many other work projects.

Between tours to Mexico, the men built buildings at the conference grounds. It wasn't long until we outgrew the brick house and put up a large building in which to hold meetings. We also held concerts every Saturday night, importing musicians some nights and using our local talent other nights. Many of these retirees had good voices and others played instruments. We soon had a band going with all kinds of instruments, conducted by Zeral himself.

More and more people heard of the conference grounds. They looked us up and came in travel trailers, and others bought life-time lots for mobile homes, until we had hundreds of retirees living on the property during the winter months. We called it "Bibleville Conference Grounds," after the name of the conference grounds in Boca Raton, Florida, which was called "Bible Town." Since our property was smaller, we named it "Bibleville" (or, little Bible town). More buildings were built for offices, laundry rooms, showers, craft rooms, shops, and a large auditorium to house our conferences and concerts. Our concerts drew huge crowds and we sometimes had to turn people away for lack of seating.

At the same time, the work of TIME Ministries grew. During the summer months, we were taking hundreds of teens and their sponsors into Mexico for a mission experience.

Of all the young people who came during the summer, one young man named Douglas Gibson returned again and again and fell in love with Pastor

Juan's oldest daughter, Noemi. Recognizing his ability to lead, Zeral soon trained him to direct the groups.

At this time, we also made contact with the pastor in the Dominican Republic and felt led to begin taking groups there for a different kind of mission's experience. In the meantime, we hired a director for the Bible Conference grounds and moved to Salem, Oregon (Zeral's hometown) and took the TIME Ministries' office with us.

Coming Full Circle

And this gospel of the kingdom will
be preached in the whole world as a
testimony to all nations, and then the
end will come.

Matthew 24:14

We took our first group to the Dominican Republic in 1992 and began working with Pastor Rudy De la Cruz. This is the same young man who was saved as an eight-year-old boy. He was now pastoring the church we began in Santo Domingo back in 1952-56. Pastor Rudy was beginning a new church plant in an apartment building in the area of Santo Domingo called "Sanchez la Fe." This building was owned by his father-in-law, who was living in New York at the time. The carport of this building (8' wide x 48' feet long) was being used for services.

At the far end of the carport was a very small kitchen, a bathroom and another room. There was also a small living room and a bedroom with bath to the side of the carport. After searching the area and inquiring about the use of a school, Pastor Rudy offered to house our first group using this apartment building. We bought foam mattresses and laid them on the floor in the back room for the girls and put the guys on the roof of the second floor. Zeral made two wooden folding tables that we set up in the carport at mealtime, which doubled as our dining room.

During services, chairs were set up in the carport for the congregation. Only a curtain divided this room from the tiny kitchen. The furnishings in the kitchen included a gas stove, a very small refrigerator, a sink and a few overhead cupboards. Four doorways opened off this room: one to the backyard, one to the girls' bedroom, one to the bathroom, and the curtain that led into the main room. Traffic was heavy through the kitchen at all times. As I mentioned, the boys slept on the roof. The mattresses had to be brought down each morning in case it rained that day. And if the rain came at night, the boys would pick up their mattresses and run down two flights of stairs and knock on our door to be let in. In one group, there was a sleepwalker, so the guys had to tie a rope around his leg to keep him from walking off the roof in his sleep.

First Chapel built in San Pedro, Dominican Republic

The apartment building was right on the street. In order for the work projects to take place, they had to haul the lumber to the roof and then lower the panels for the chapels using ropes. One crew worked right on the street.

The church was growing and in need of larger facilities. Zeral and Pastor Rudy spent all of their free time looking for an empty lot that was suitable for a church and at a price that we could afford. At the time the first chapel was built, no lot was found, so Rudy decided to give the chapel to a church in the town of San Pedro de Marcoris. This congregation had bought an empty lot and needed a building. The house they had been renting was no longer available.

Zeral encouraged Rudy to begin looking farther out for property. A young man across the street had an old car that he offered to drive them around in. Eventually, they found a new suburb in Villa Mella where lots were being sold at a price we could handle. Zeral offered to pay the small down payment if the church could handle the monthly payments.

We continued to house the groups in the apartment during the next year. These groups began to build our first building on the new property. By the summer of 1994, we purchased a large tent (40' x 60') and erected it on the new property for services. In the meantime, we built several chapels to house the groups and set up a kitchen of sorts. We still had no water or electricity. The first group of men we housed on the property used the neighbors' showers and bathrooms. We carried all of our water in gallon jugs for the kitchen. Over time, we made improvements. Soon the tent was able to be used for building the chapels. A cistern was put in and we bought water by the truckload to fill it.

Zeral's health began to deteriorate in 1994. He suffered a light heart attack and was hospitalized. He recovered and was able to function normally with medication. Then because of poor circulation, his legs began to ache. But he never considered stopping work. We continued to travel to advertise the ministry and to raise funds and groups for building chapels.

By the summer of 1996, his condition worsened enough so that he would only supervise the work team for awhile and then return to our room to lie down. Gradually, pains in the chest area increased. Finally he agreed to go to a clinic to see a cardiologist where he was treated and then released. A few days later, continued pain convinced us to return to the clinic. We were told that he needed more than what the doctors in the Dominican Republic could give him. On August 15 of 1996, we made arrangements with our insurance company to send a plane to fly him to Miami. He suffered several more heart attacks in Miami and they decided to operate. A few days after surgery, his kidneys failed and he passed on to glory on August 31.

During the last days in Miami, my two daughters and son flew to be with him. We shipped his body to Salem, Oregon, where we held a memorial service and buried him in the cemetery there on September 4, 1996. Naturally, I was deeply saddened after losing a partner of 53 years and wondered just what I was to do now. He was my life. The more I thought about it and prayed about it, I considered the fact that missions was the only thing I knew. I knew the language and I had a good monthly income. Why not just continue doing what I knew best?

By January of 1997, I was ready to return to the Dominican Republic and take up my duties as Interim Director and kitchen supervisor. Bill Malehorn had joined TIME Ministries and was sent to be my assistant. After working all of my life alongside Zeral, it was very difficult to adjust to working with a new and different personality. Poor Bill had to adjust to my telling him how to do things. He was new to missions and to the customs of the people, and I was not a very patient teacher. But we learned to work together and became good friends.

Zeral and I (as foreigners in the Dominican Republic) looked to Pastor Rudy and his wife, Patria, for continual advice and help with the local customs. We worked to make sure that we were culturally correct in our dealings with the people. It was natural for me to continue to look to Rudy and Patria for advice and help. There was never a problem or situation that Patria couldn't solve. She continued to keep the financial records as she had done for Zeral. This was very important because I was not good at keeping good records or at being organized. I would never have succeeded in my new role without Patria and her help.

As the work of TIME Ministries grew, and more and more groups became interested in building chapels for the Dominican people, and as the ministry of Pastor Rudy and his church (Iglesia Bautista Quisqueyana) grew, we realized the need for our own headquarters. The church needed more space and TIME Ministries needed more adequate dorms, dining room, kitchen, and meeting rooms. After a lot of prayer, many consultants, much time spent in looking for property, and with the advice of Pastor Rudy, Board members, Director of TIME Ministries, and friends, it was decided to purchase the property next to the church. Since TIME had no available funds, we looked to God to provide. I sent out letters asking for prayer. God laid it on the hearts of his people and they began to give toward this project. Soon the money for the property was supplied and we bought the three available lots.

Rudy took care of negotiating for the best price, making all of the arrangements, and completing the necessary paperwork.

A friend in Arizona offered to match all funds raised up to $70,000. We were able to raise about $35,000 and, with the matching funds, we had $70,000. An architect who was a member of Rudy's church was contracted to draw the plans. I took these plans before the Board of TIME Ministries for their approval. It was to be a three-story building, covering the three lots (50' x 50') with dorms on the third floor, kitchen and dining room on the second floor, and shop and offices on the first floor. It would house our complete ministry. It all seemed like an impossible dream.

Soon the foundation was begun. Most of the heavy work was contracted out, but many groups of adults lent a hand in tying steel, laying blocks, carrying sand, and many other things. The funds continued to come in and we were able to construct the building. Since I know nothing about construction, I looked to Rudy and Patria for help. Patria literally became the contractor. Her dad was a contractor and she learned from him. She handled all the money, bought all material, hired, fired, and supervised all the paid workers. On every decision, she would consult me first. The people have named the edifice "Dorretta's Building" but the name should be "Patria's Building." In July of 2006, a dedication of the building was held to praise God for his magnificent provision.

My youngest daughter, Sharon, left her job in 2001 and joined TIME Ministries to work with me in the Dominican. She remembered a lot of her Spanish and was a great people person. She loved to drive and really enjoyed the challenge of driving in the heavy, crazy traffic of the Dominican. Her job was to coordinate the ministry part of each group. She was able to preview each presentation, such as drama, special songs, testimonies, and puppets, beforehand. It was a real loss when she felt led to resign after two years and return to her job in Salem, Oregon.

My oldest daughter, Joanna Berry, was promoted to Vice President of International Ministries of South Texas Children's Home. She is also the Director of their Family Counseling Center. Since she speaks fluent Spanish and is well acquainted with the Dominican Republic having been raised there, she felt it was a good place to begin. She immediately planned a tour to the DR for the Director of the South Texas Children's Home and a few other employees. They were very favorably impressed. Thus began the blessing of having my oldest daughter working together with me in the ministry.

I felt led to move back to Texas in 2004 to live near my daughter, Joanna and her husband, John Berry. I joined First Baptist Church in Corpus Christi, Texas. The move has been a very difficult adjustment because I miss my friends in Salem, Oregon. After three years, I feel that I'm only beginning to become acquainted with people at the church. I was asked to be Facilitator of their Women's Missionary Group and I have enjoyed serving in that capacity. I was able to present my ministry and the work of TIME Ministries on June 4, 2008 and felt a real rapport with the ladies.

A Call to Missions

Whoever has my commands and obeys them, he is the one who loves me. He who loves me will be loved by my Father, and I too will love him and show myself to him.

John 14:21

Never once have I considered my experiences to be so overwhelming as to wish I had never answered the call to be a missionary. If I could go back and have the opportunity to choose my life's work, I would gladly choose the way that I took. I am not a person with grandiose visions of doing a great work for God. My goal was not to complete 60 years serving God on the mission field. My goal was to please God in my daily walk with Him, to obey His Word to the best of my ability, to follow His will wherever that took me. The hardest part for me at times was to know what His will was. But when His will was revealed to me, I wanted to obey Him.

I discovered I could trust Him to take care of me and to meet my every need. Not once were Zeral and I without food to eat, a bed to sleep in, or clothes to wear.

As it is written in Matthew 6:33: "But seek first his kingdom and his righteousness and all these things will be given to you as well."

In writing down my experiences, I hope to leave you with this challenge:

If God is calling you to the mission field, follow His will for your life. By obeying God, you will be blessed; God is always faithful. He doesn't promise that everything will go well for you. He gives us trials in our lives to teach us perseverance and to teach us to lean on Him. But, as He promises, He will go with you wherever you go (Joshua 1:9) and will never forsake you (Joshua 1:5).

May God richly bless you in your service to Him!

Dorretta Brown

Afterword by Linda Scheele

How then, can they call on the one they have not believed in? And how can they believe in the one of whom they have not heard? And how can they hear without someone preaching to them? And how can they preach unless they are sent? . . .

Romans 10:14-15

The life of a missionary—Dorretta's life, for example—appears at first glance to be a simple life, yet it is not so simple when compared to our lives. We skim through the pages of Dorretta's life and see a wife and mother at work behind the scenes. She tells God that she is willing to serve as the best mother and wife that she can be. She tells us, the readers, that she merely did the "grunt" work. And, in fact, we see her doing ordinary things like caring for her husband and children, cooking, sewing, and teaching Bible stories. However, we also see the realities of living—at times—in third-world conditions.

With a soft voice and sweet smile, Dorretta humbly tells us of warming a baby bottle on the manifold of a car, of tarantulas in the outhouse, of children almost dying of Cholera, of a husband being stoned with rocks, of finding poisonous centipedes in her son's bed, of eating meat that had been covered in flies in an open-air market. And, even when she was honored at a Mexican dinner by being given the goat's head, Dorretta maintained her composure and politely accepted, asking her host if she could take it home to eat later.

Dorretta's life was anything but simple and definitely not ordinary, yet we see in her testimony that God uses ordinary people to accomplish His purposes. Despite the inconveniences, the sacrifices, and the dangers of living in third-world conditions, Dorretta and Zeral followed God's will for their lives. Humbly, they accepted a lifetime of service. They trusted God to provide, and God never let them down; our God is a faithful God.

We experience a snapshot of missionary life when we go camping or go on a short-term mission trip to a different country. But, it is in the tediousness of living day in and day out without conveniences like running water, electricity, or modern bathroom facilities that truly tests our faith.

After our camping trip, or short-term mission trip, we return to our weather-proof homes, comfortable beds and chairs, closet full of clothes, cupboards and refrigerators full of food, and our busy lives. We have access to phones, televisions, radios, music, cars, stocked grocery stores, fast-food restaurants, disposable diapers, libraries, computers and Internet. Our days are full of activities and events with family and friends, like birthday parties, holidays, and sporting events. We live in a country where excess is commonplace.

We are all part of the body of Christ and "we are God's workmanship, created in Christ Jesus to do good works, which God prepared in advance for us to do" (Ephesians 2:10). We may not be called—or even want to go—to the mission field. Some of us don't want to "step out of that boat." But we can show our support for these brothers and sisters who are willing to serve God, away from the comforts and conveniences of home here in the states, away from family and friends—year after year.

I want to encourage everyone to support missionaries through giving financially, regularly praying for them, and sending care packages to them. Thank God for people like Dorretta, who are willing to serve on the front lines of God's Kingdom work. Her life was and continues to be one of obedience to God.

To this day, Dorretta continues to serve God in her church, in the Dominican Republic, and wherever she is called.

It was my honor and privilege to work with Dorretta on her story.

Made in the USA
San Bernardino, CA
05 August 2014